JAGUAR

An Illustrated History
of the
World's Most Elegant Car

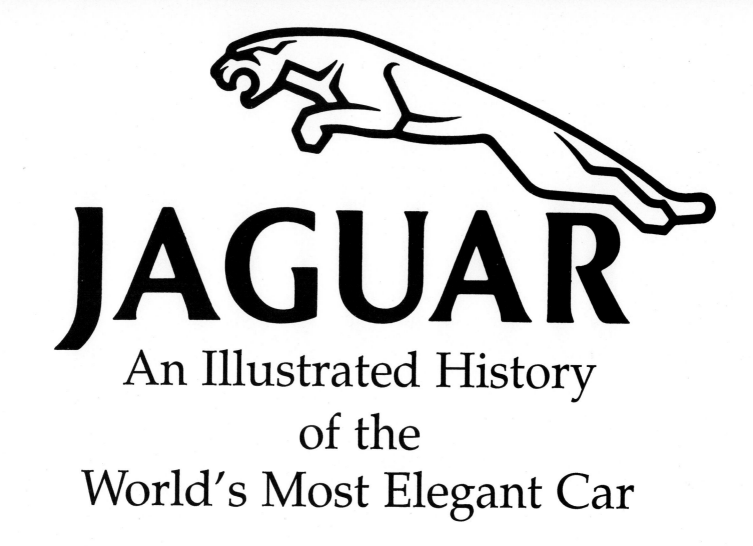

JAGUAR

An Illustrated History
of the
World's Most Elegant Car

Text by
Roger Hicks

CRESCENT BOOKS

NEW YORK

Acknowledgements

The publishers would like to offer their special thanks to the following, who
provided the cars and assistance without which this book would not have been
possible:
Will Athawes
D. Birch
John Blake
Geoff Brooks
Ron Buch
Paul Cizek
Gordon Clark
B.R. Cracknell
Richard Embling
Les Eveson
Melvyn Fancy
Peter Hall
L. Harper
A.G. Hendry
Alan Hodges and staff at Jaguar Cars – Coventry
Willy Khan
Bill Lake
Peter and Dulce Lawson
Peter McCabe
Harold Meyer
Alan Minchin
Guy Salmon Ltd.
A.W. Smith
Brian Wagstaff
Tom Walker
Particular thanks to Alan Hames who compiled the list of cars to be
photographed.

Featuring the photography of Neil Sutherland

CLB 2292
© 1989 Colour Library Books Ltd, Godalming, Surrey, England
Printed and bound in Hong Kong by Leefung Asco Printers Ltd
1989 edition published by Crescent Books, distributed by Crown Publishers, Inc.
ISBN 0 517 67413 0
h g f e d c b a

Dep. Leg. B. 17.217/83

Most cars are defined by the people who buy them. Certain Italian cars, for example, cater to the playboy image. Rolls Royces are still used in socialist cartoons, where the bloated plutocrat smokes a fat cigar and grinds the faces of the poor; and vintage Bentleys are in the Bulldog Drummond tradition of heroes who rescue maidens in distress and the British Empire from destruction with equal aplomb.

The Jaguar, on the other hand, has appealed to so many people with so many cars that it is not really possible to characterise it in this way: it is the car which bears the image, not the buyers. This means that while in some ways the Jaguar image is very clear, in others it is very diffuse. What can one make of a car which appeals to royalty and politicians as a limousine; to bank robbers as a getaway car (a cynic might draw parallels . . .); to high-powered executives as a means of driving (or, sometimes, being driven) very quickly about the country to look after their business interests; and to the makers of porno films as the 'Wardour Street Rolls'? A car which on top of all that dominated Le Mans in the 1950s.

Nobody is quite sure when the slogan 'Grace . . . Pace . . . Space' was coined, but it sums up the appeal of the Jaguar better than anything else. Not all Jaguars (nor their forerunners, Swallow and SS) have exhibited all three characteristics; but where one (or even two) of these desirable qualities has been missing, the augmentation of the others has usually been such that the omission is freely forgiven. For example, the 160 mph performance of the D-type Jaguar, coupled with its purposeful sleekness, makes the extremely cramped racing interior irrelevant; and at the other end of the scale, the looks and appointments of the SS1 (at least in its second series) mean that the lack of performance is merely regrettable; it is not particularly important. It was really only in the post-war saloons, culminating in the XJ6/XJ12, that grace, pace and space really came together in a big way.

What is certain is that almost all Jaguars have caught the spirit of their times in a very special way; they have always expressed the aspirations, perhaps the dreams, of many, and they have also been eminently affordable – at least by comparison with anything else with similar looks, specification, or performance.

Very roughly, there have been three kinds of Jaguar; the sports cars, the small sporting saloons, and the large saloons (which have also had very sporting performance, but which seem slightly out-of-place when described as 'sports saloons').

The small sporting saloon was for years the mainstay of Jaguar. 'Small' is of course a relative term, and is merely used to distinguish them from big saloons, or limousines; they were certainly a good deal larger than a modern 'mini' car. For speed and comfort they were always in the forefront, except in the very earliest SS days when speed was only slightly ahead of other cars of comparable size. The original pre-war 2½ litre and 3½ litre SS Jaguars, and their immediately post-war brethren, founded this tradition; but it was the original 2.4 and (especially) 3.4 XK-engined small saloons which brought it to its peak. Apart from their obvious appeal to anyone who wanted a practical car with excellent handling and performance, these attributes endeared them alike to police and to villains who wanted a getaway car; the latter were particularly helped by the low cost of a new Jaguar, which meant that a second-hand example could be picked up very cheaply indeed – or, because of the considerable numbers in which they were made, simply stolen. They were also successful in production car racing, and they were a useful reward for the company man as a rather special company car.

The larger saloons were a phenomenon of the late 1940s and 1950s, though they lingered on well into the 1960s. Still with quite remarkable performance (and frightening fuel consumption to match, if they were driven hard), they appealed to all kinds of people: Her Majesty Queen Elizabeth the Queen Mother had a Mk. VII, and its nickname of the 'Wardour Street Rolls' has already been mentioned; it was certainly popular at many levels in show business, and especially in the film trade. The Mk. X was the last monster Jaguar, though the S-type furnished an intermediate step between this and the small saloons. They were used by diplomats, as upper-echelon chauffeur-driven cars for those who did not warrant Rolls Royces, and elsewhere.

The two strands – large and small saloon – came together in 1968 in the XJ6, which appealed to almost all the buyers already mentioned, plus quite a few more who saw it as Jaguar's coming of age. It became one of the standard company cars for senior executives (the chairman would drive an XJ12); politicians rode in it; police drove it in bright colours, as the 'flying jam sandwich'; and of course, the baddies still stole it as a getaway car.

5

It is the sports cars, though, which have the most romantic associations. The SS100 is the ultimate 'cad's car' (known more vulgarly as a 'tart trap'), driven by the kind of young man who would like to think of himself as (and sometimes became) a dashing RAF air ace; for many, it summarises the sports cars of the 1930s, even though so few were made.

The XK120 was much more of a competition car, if only because more were made and more could afford to compete in the 1950s, but it was also much favoured by starlets and as a present for wives. It also gained a firm following in the United States as a 'personal' car, as did its successors the XK140 and XK150. The E-type was the XK120 all over again, though the jargon of the time also recognised it as the ultimate 'bird puller' – the 1960s equivalent of a 'tart trap'.

The C-type and D-type, of course, were 'dream cars': built as racers for the road (or, in the case of the XK-SS, primarily as road cars); even now, they exercise their magic. How many children who pushed a D-type model car up and down the carpet have since bought one?

The only car which is a puzzle is the XJ-S. It does not seem to appeal to the traditional Jaguar market, though it does have a significant place in the 'busy executive' market – the kind of man who wants a status symbol without going to the length of a real sports car, and who is very unlikely indeed ever to take advantage of the car's performance except perhaps in a straight line on a deserted motorway when late for a meeting. It offers performance similar to an Aston Martin, Ferrari, or Maserati – but unlike them, it does not spend a large portion of its life off the road being serviced. But it is the only puzzle, and Jaguar cannot be too worried about it, as they seem to sell them fast enough, so perhaps it is as well to go on to the cars themselves, and their origins.

Bill Walmsley was an ardent motorcyclist. He served in the Great War (where he was wounded in the foot) and, when it was all over, he made a living reconditioning and selling ex-WD Triumph motorcycles: all the combatant governments had gone in for mechanisation in a big way, and there was a lot of surplus machinery about. As a sideline, he also made a very elegant Zeppelin-shaped side-car, made of polished aluminium, which attracted a great deal of attention wherever it was seen.

Across the road from Walmsley lived another young man – about ten years younger, in fact, than Walmsley. His name was William Lyons, and he was just twenty when he saw the commercial potential of Walmsley's side-cars. In 1922, at Lyon's instigation, they formed the Swallow Sidecar Company.

Swallow Sidecars were certainly elegant, and they were seen on the side of many leading motorcycles of the day – George Brough's Brough Superior, or the imported Harley Davidson. With a man like Lyons, though, expansion was inevitable, and it was not long before they moved into the business of rebodying motor cars. By 1926, they were already advertising themselves as the Swallow Sidecar and Coachbuilding Company, and in 1927 they were rebodying the humble Austin Seven to look distinctly more sporting, as well as painting it in a range of colours which took it out of mourning and into the bright life of the 1920s.

This sort of exercise was by no means unusual; after all, Cecil Kimber's rebodied Morrises were sold under the Morris Garages label, which was abbreviated to become another famous *marque*: MG. What was unusual was the skill and aplomb with which the rebodying was carried out; the cars may have been small and inexpensive, but they were luxurious and (by the standards of the day) elegant.

Others followed the Austin Seven Swallow: in the same year there was a Morris Cowley Swallow, and in 1929 Lyons got hold of some obsolescent FIAT 509A chassis and bodied those: the transformation from the Gothic perpendicular of the standard body to the rather more rakish lines of the Swallow offering makes it very clear why even FIAT in Britain catalogued the proprietary alternative. In 1929/1930, there was also a Swift Swallow, though this was to be short-lived, as Swift went into receivership in 1931. Also at the 1929 Motor Show with the Swift Swallow was the Standard Swallow.

The latter was on a Standard Nine four-cylinder chassis, but the standard Standard radiator (one of the difficulties with a car named Standard!) was of such vintage appearance that it was replaced in 1930 with a special Swallow-designed version, which looked a good deal racier. In 1931 the body was remodelled again, but it was in May 1931 that the fledgeling Swallow made its next big step forward: the adoption of the six-cylinder Standard Ensign chassis, the first six-cylinder Swallow saloon.

The Standard connection was to prove most important, but before we return to it, mention should be made of the Wolseley Hornet Swallow, announced in January 1931. These already attractive little cars looked even sportier with Swallow coachwork, and at only £30 more than the standard Hornet, they were very good value. With their six cylinders, these were the first Swallow sixes of all, but they were all open cars.

All of these cars were produced in comparatively small numbers: the Standard Ensign Swallow, for example, ran to fifty-six cars, the Fiat Swallow to something similar, and perhaps twice as many Swift Swallows were made. What is important to realise, too, is that they were in no way 'souped up'. The Swallow bodywork was often lighter than the original, which made some difference, and the cars may have looked rather sportier, but no modifications were made either to engine or to chassis. The terms 'sports car' in those days was more a declaration of intent, or even an advertising description, than anything very meaningful – very much as 'GT' became in the 1960s.

The first step in the evolution of a real Swallow sports car came in 1931, when Lyons persuaded Standard to make a special chassis just for Swallow, still bearing the Standard six-cylinder side-valve engine. This was bodied as the SS1, originally seen at the 1931 Motor Show. It was very much in the style of the SSK Mercedes, with an immensely long bonnet in proportion to the wheelbase – over half the length of the car! As originally styled by Lyons, there would have been virtually no room for the passengers, so Walmsley took advantage of Lyon's enforced absence due to an appendix operation to raise the roofline considerably. Lyons was furious when he saw it, and called it a 'conning tower'; and it is hard to disagree with him. Even so, the admittedly sycophantic press of the day were overwhelmed and praised the car to the heavens.

In 1932, the SS1 was restyled more to Lyons liking, and became a very much better vehicle. The chassis was underslung at the rear, and the quality of the whole car was improved dramatically: buyers of the original SS1 soon found that bits fell off, doors dropped, and sundry other faults manifested themselves. Even so, the SS1 was scarcely a sports saloon: with a 2054cc side-valve engine delivering 45 bhp gross to haul a 26cwt car, it could hardly be so. Even with the '20 hp' (taxation horsepower, of course) option, there was only 62 bhp on tap; this was later improved to 53/68 bhp in 1934 and to 62/70 bhp in 1935.

Nevertheless, the SS1 was significant for several reasons. One was that it marked the emergence of Swallow as a manufacturer of cars, rather than a coach works. A second was that it clearly showed the way that Swallow (later Jaguar) was going to go; and the third was that it represented quite extraordinary value for money. It was billed as 'The car with the £1,000 look . . . which only costs £310'.

This was achieved in many ways, but the most important was by what would nowadays be called 'production engineering'. By ingenious re-thinking and streamlining of traditional coachbuilding techniques, by a determined policy of self-sufficiency and improvisation, and by an acute awareness of economy, William Lyons kept the prices of his cars to the very minimum. Only rarely was this at the expense of quality; though there have been many points in Jaguars which could have been better executed, they have rarely been inferior to any other cars on the market, and when new techniques become widespread – such as wax-injection of box members subject to rust – Jaguar is normally as quick to adopt them as anyone. The real skill lies in simplicity, and in a refusal to change for change's sake: a proven feature is always used until it is definitely obsolete, and

even (on occasion) for some time afterwards.

The SS1 was available as a saloon, as a rather odd-looking 'Airline' saloon with 1930s streamlining, as an open four-seater, as a Coupé, and as a Drophead Coupé; of course, in those days, such body variations were rather easier to achieve, as cars were chassis built. Although Jaguar always saw themselves as saloon car producers (and still do), it also spawned the SS90, a short-chassis version with two-seater bodywork. This had the '20 hp' engine, by this time delivering about 70 bhp (gross), and weighed only about 22½ cwt; still not sporting by modern standards, but pretty good by the standards of the day, with a top speed approaching 90 and a 0-60 time of well under 20 seconds – all for £395.

Incidentally, the meaning of the initials 'SS' was always carefully left open. Those who wished (especially Black, at Standard) could read it as Standard Swallow; others could take it as Standard Sports, or even Super Sport, and there was always the precedent of George Brough's SS80 and SS100 motorcycles.

Announced at the same time as the SS1 was the SS2, a 'baby brother' to the SS1 based on the Standard Little Nine; it was extremely unexciting by comparison with the SS1, with a 1006cc side-valve engine delivering only 28 bhp, but it marked the last of the essentially rebodied bought-in chassis; in 1933, both the chassis and the engine were changed, but it was always very much the poor relation next to the SS1.

With the advent of the SS90, it becomes appropriate to consider the two separate strands of Jaguar development separately: first the sports cars (which are covered in this chapter under the heading 'Pace'), and then the saloons, which are considered next under the heading 'Space'.

The car which most people automatically associate with the name Jaguar before the war is the SS100. It was introduced in 1935, and was the first car to bear the name 'Jaguar': Lyons selected the word from a list of animal, fish, and bird names prepared by his publicity department, and was given permission to use it by Armstrong Siddeley who had used it for an aero engine in the Great War.

The SS100 Jaguar was derived from the SS90, though there were many changes to the body and trim: perhaps one of the most obvious was the adoption of huge P100 headlamps. Far more important, though, was the new engine.

It was still based on the old seven-bearing, six-cylinder 2663cc Standard '20 hp' engine, but in place of the side-valves, there was now a new Weslake-designed overhead-valve head, which allowed well over 100 bhp (about 104 bhp on the original test example) to be extracted. With only 23 cwt to propel, the performance was pretty good by the standards of twenty years later; at the time, it was superb.

The '100' was something of a misnomer (unlike Brough, who guaranteed an SS100 to 100 mph in writing), but it could hit about 95 mph under favourable conditions, and the 0-60 time was a mere 12½ seconds. In late 1937, though, when the new season's cars were announced, the SS100 grew to 3485cc by a combination of boring and stroking. Weight went up very little, but power went up to 125 bhp, allowing a genuine 100 mph (with the screen folded, in sporting fashion) and a 0-60 mph time of around ten seconds. Understandably, the press was overwhelmed!

We can see here a glimpse of how Lyons managed to produce so much car for the money – only £445. The chassis was not new, and the new engine was strictly a development of the previous units. This technique of getting the maximum possible use out of everything is very characteristic of Jaguar – as we shall see when we come to the legendary XK engine.

The war, of course, put paid to practical motor-car development for some time – though the story of Lyons and others at Jaguar discussing future plans whilst on fire-watch duty is well known. During the war, Jaguar made all kinds of things, including about 10,000 sidecars for the military, and were involved in such projects as repairing Whitley bombers and building Gloster Meteor bodies. After the war, work went ahead on several fronts; to begin with, various pre-war saloons (but not sports cars) were reintroduced as a stopgap, but work centred around a new double-overhead-cam engine. A four cylinder version, the XJ, was used by Goldie Gardner in his 1948 record-breaking run at 176.694 mph in an MG special (very special, with a 2-litre 4-cylinder Jaguar engine), but Jaguar did not consider the 'four' to be smooth enough for the Jaguar image.

Although new in many ways, the OHC XK engine (as the 3.4 litre 'six' was known) owed a lot to the original seven-bearing Standard design of the late 1920s. Enormously strong and free from the crankshaft whip which had afflicted so many 'sixes' (even Rolls Royce at one time!), in its XK incarnation it delivered a basic, reliable 160 bhp, or an equally reliable 180 bhp in the 'special equipment' form which was offered in about 1951.

This unit was intended to power the new generation of Jaguar saloons, but – almost as an afterthought, and as a way of seeing how the new engine would perform in customers' hands – the XK120 was built around the new engine. Its birth was an incredibly quick process, with the body designed in a matter of weeks. It was based on a cut-down Mk. V saloon chassis (of which more later), and Lyons worked in his usual way: the prototype was made up as he went along, with a skilled metal-worker forming the panels under his direction until he was satisfied that they looked right. The original XK120 models were made in aluminium, partly because it was easy to work (and the production run envisaged was very short), and partly because aluminium was more readily available than steel in those miserable post-war years; the Land Rover owes its corrosion-resistant body to the same exigencies. The first car is said to have been built from scratch in about six weeks, and it was first displayed to the public at the 1948 Motor Show.

The flood of orders which followed soon made Jaguar realise that they would have to go over to a pressed steel body, and although a steady trickle of aluminium-on-ash (very traditional!) bodies left the works in 1949/1950, they were replaced by the steel-bodied cars (which were about 1 cwt heavier) in 1950. Nevertheless, it was a production aluminium-bodied XK120 which pulled the magnificent stunt at Jabbeke of driving at just over 132 mph in the two-way flying mile, and then driving past the assembled journalists in top gear at 5 mph – which effectively dispelled all doubts about the out-and-out performance of the vehicle, and about its tractability. The latter was perhaps the biggest surprise, for many expected such a potent vehicle, travelling at racer-like speeds, to need a resident mechanic in the front seat and to behave erratically in traffic – much as pre-war Bugattis had done.

At the same time, the XK100 (with the two-litre four-cylinder engine) was announced, but it was never made; the few engines which were made (perhaps as many as 50) were used for research, for testing ('Lofty' England drove an XK100/120), or simply scrapped.

The XK120 had a few faults, notably rather fade-prone brakes, but they were generally agreed to be trivial when compared with its advantages. A fixed-head coupé joined the two-seater in 1951, and a drop-head coupé in 1953.

By 1954, the usual clamour for yet more power was heeded: the XK140 was announced. It had slightly less spartan lines than the XK120, a fair bit of which was due to the massive bumpers needed for American parking techniques (America had taken to the XK in a big way), but whereas the usual 'special equipment' engines for the XK120 delivered 190 bhp, this was the *standard* figure for the XK140; the SE engine now delivered 210 bhp (although this had been available for the last XK120s, too). The car was a couple of hundredweight heavier, though, and although the 0-60 time of the SE two-seater was now under 8½ seconds, the '140' did not refer to the top speed in the way that the '120' did; without overdrive, top speed was only about 1 mph greater, though with overdrive it could just about manage 130 mph.

The XK140 was basically a more civilised version of the XK120 – a slippery path which almost all manufacturers of 'real' sports cars have wandered down, usually losing performance in the process – and the XK150, announced in 1957, was a clear case of 'more of the same'. Fortunately, despite another 100 lb. or so extra weight, even the original 210 bhp XK150s were not significantly worse performers than the XK140, and they were very much more comfortable. Also, with disc brakes, they were very much safer! When the faithful XK engine was bored out to 3.8 litres in 1959, it was also made to deliver 220 bhp (standard) and 265 bhp (special), which knocked another second or so off the 0-60 time and brought 140 mph at least within sight: contemporary road tests all mention figures in the 130s, sometimes the high 130s.

If you wanted more speed, of course, you could always have it; from about 1951 onwards, Jaguar were producing factory information sheets on performance improvement, as well as selling "accessories" such as lumpier camshafts and even big-valve heads. With this kind of attention the XK120/140/150 figures were on the low side; the cars could be made to go a good deal faster than their names would suggest. One thing which did suffer with increasing weight and greater power, though, was fuel consumption. An XK120 could return between 15 and 25 miles to the (imperial) gallon, but even an unmodified XK150S 3.8 would be hard put to return 20 mpg, and hard or incompetent driving could get it down to 13-14 mpg. This was assuming perfect tune: if the three 2″ SU carburetters were badly out of synchronisation, single-figure fuel consumption was not impossible.

By the 1960s, though, the XK-series was looking distinctly vintage. Strange as it may seem now, they were not regarded as 'off the shelf classics', but simply as cars that had outlived their time. The 1950s and 1960s were a bad time for this, of course: the Triumph TR-series, which were produced principally to spite Jaguar, (Black and Lyons fell out after the war, and Black decided to use his newly acquired Triumph concern to compete with Jaguar) are generally reckoned to have deteriorated steadily as the TR-number increased. Only Morgan kept the faith.

Their replacement was to be as far ahead of its time as the XK120 had been in its day. The unashamedly phallic E-type Jaguar was announced to the public in 1961. It broke with the XK-series by being of unitary construction, but once again the most powerful engine of the old series became the standard engine for the new. Weight was down to 24 cwt – a saving of a quarter of a ton on the last of the XK150 models – and 265 bhp was enough to propel this astonishingly low-slung (under four feet with the hood up) and surprisingly short (only 14′ 7½″ in its original form) car at very close to 150 mph; the fixed-head car actually exceeded this figure on road test, and fuel consumption figures on test were in the 18-20 mpg bracket.

Once again, the press raved. There was an amazing new independent rear suspension, superb handling (though many people strengthened the sills for competition use), and once again the kind of looks which summarised the dreams of a generation. On looks alone, the E-type Jaguar was surely one of the most thrilling cars ever made: the same was true on performance alone. What is more, by making it in series-production numbers, sharing tried-and-tested parts with Jaguar saloon cars (and there are few parts more tried-and-tested than the XK engine!) Lyons managed to keep the price down to believable levels; on introduction, it was just over £2000 in the UK, and it was to dip briefly under that before beginning the long climb which characterised car prices in the late 1960s and throughout the 1970s.

The engine was increased to 4.2 litres in 1964, and although overall rated horsepower did not increase, torque did; but, again, the weight increased to just over 25 cwt, so performance was very little altered. From then on, the E-type grew steadily more obese. The biggest change was arguably in 1966, when it was 'stretched' to a 2+2: at nine inches longer, and two inches higher, plus *another* couple of hundredweight to bring the dry weight in sight of 28 cwt, the coupé still looked graceful and lithe – but it was the grace and litheness of a pregnant cat, rather than a hunting one! On top of all this, a three-speed 'slush box' was made an option; the combined effect of all this was to add about two seconds to the 0-60 mph time, and to knock about 12-15 mph off the top speed. Even then, a car with a 0-60 time of 8.9 seconds and a top speed of 136 mph is hardly slow, especially when equipped the way the Jaguar was; but the purists were unhappy.

In 1971, however, another variant on the E-type was announced. In place of the long-serving straight six, there was another truly impressive engine: a 5.3 litre V12. The DIN bhp figure was 272, corresponding to way over 300 bhp under the old 'gross' rating, and the torque was a truly spectacular 304 lb ft (DIN) as compared with the 283 lb ft (gross) of the 'six'. Inevitably, the weight went up yet again, this time to 28.8 cwt dry, but even so there were 0-60 mph times in the low sixes and a top speed in the high 140s. Even in 2+2 form, the speed was over 140 mph, but once again the fuel consumption figures told their own story: 14-15 miles to the imperial gallon, or a still more alarming 11-12 miles to the U.S. gallon.

The V12 was the result of a long series of experiments with engines other than the straight six, and even when it entered production, the machine tools were selected on the basis of being able to machine a V8 as well as a V12. In the end, though, the V12 was selected for a number of reasons. Prestige and mystique were not least among them, as Lyons was always keenly aware of any selling advantage, but the magnificent smoothness of a V12 (which has almost equal firing intervals throughout a revolution) and the immense power which it could deliver were also decisive. The final design, as produced, had a single overhead cam to each bank of cylinders: a double-DOHC design was contemplated (and even tested), but rejected on the grounds of cost, complexity, noise, and the fact that it was in any case unnecessary; new developments in 'flat-head' engines meant that enough power could be extracted from the simple design for any reasonable or indeed foreseeable occasion. Of course, the unfortunate Americans were burdened with emission control equipment which reduced power and increased fuel consumption still further; the 1974 American specification V12 took eight whole seconds to reach 60 mph, had a top speed of 135 mph, and got through an Imperial gallon of petrol every twelve miles (a US gallon every ten miles). To a large extent, it was the American emission regulations which made the V12 necessary; late 'non-emission' sixes were comparable in power with 'emission' V12s.

The XK-series lasted in production for eleven years, from 1949 to 1960. The E-type ran for rather longer: from 1961 to 1975. In its turn, it was replaced by another ultra-fast car, though this time without the magic Lyons touch: for the first time, an outside stylist was brought in – and it showed! Despite the 285 bhp (DIN) petrol-injected engine, and an admirably slippery shape which enabled the XJ-S to reach 153 mph (142 even in automatic guise), many – perhaps most – felt that its coupé styling had rather lost its way. Admittedly, it was not advertised so much as a sports car, but more as a GT. It was very much based on the original XJ saloon, though the wheelbase was shortened to 102″, and various little goodies like 6″ wide alloy wheels (bearing frighteningly expensive tyres!) and anti-roll bars front and rear were fitted; the handling was never in question, just the appearance. A lot of this seems to have been due to a misinterpretation of the prospective American safety legislation in the early 1970s, when it looked as if dropheads were going to be outlawed completely; many manufacturers were misled by this, which put drophead development back half a decade. Sadly, though, a great deal seems also to have been due to an over-willingness to please the American market. It is often said that to an American, a sports car automatically means a foreign car; and as the XJ-S did not look foreign enough, it was not regarded as sporting enough. One cannot help feeling that it would never have happened under Sir William Lyons (he was knighted in 1956).

Carping aside, though, there is no doubt that the XJ-S is a very fine car. It has had more than its share of quality control problems, but what car from British Leyland (apart from perhaps the Land Rover) has not? One cannot help feeling that the majority of cavils come from people who do not own one and perhaps could never afford to do so: it is easy to 'knock' something at that distance. Another source of complaints is the traditionalist – especially the traditionalist motoring writer!

Almost anyone is impressed by the cars of his youth, as they were the ones he first wanted to own; and when any reality, no matter how good, is set alongside a dream, the reality seldom stands a chance. With the latest 'HE' (high efficiency) engines, even the former complaints about the 11-14 mpg fuel consumption are much reduced: with care, 20 mpg is just about attainable, and 16-17 mpg is by no means out of the way. For a car which can transport four people, those in the back

in quite reasonable comfort, at 150 mph this is scarcely bad.

Although it was the SS100 Jaguar which caught the public imagination, and which is much better remembered today, the Jaguar name and the new OHV engine were introduced simultaneously in the 2.5 litre SS Jaguar saloon. Once again, the chassis was a stiffened SS90 type, but the bodywork was a masterpiece: finely balanced, without any of that element of parody which beset even the SS100, and blending dignity with a hint of speed in the most delightful way. The body was of steel on ash, made up of a very large number of relatively tiny panels and making considerable use of lead filler to cover up the joins; in an era when labour was cheap, and mechanisation expensive, this provided a surprisingly economical way to make up a body.

Any pre-1960 car nowadays seems to have a very high waistline when you sit in it, and this can feel rather claustrophobic. The Jaguar was no exception to the high waist, but in the front at least there is a fair amount of room; the back is another matter, and with the seats fully back, room is not all it might be. It is certainly not bad, especially when compared with any of its contemporaries, and with the improvements made in 1936 it was even better. Here, for the first time, was the sort of car that a gentleman might buy. It was not in the least raffish, and it marks the beginning of the fast Jaguar saloon for the sporting driver who wanted to enjoy his motoring but needed something a bit bigger and more practical than a sports car.

As with the SS1/SS11, there was again a 'baby' in the form of the SS Jaguar 1½ litre, with a 1608cc 4-cylinder side-valve engine delivering a very creditable 52 bhp; but next to the 2663cc OHV engine with almost double the output (102 bhp), even a weight saving of about 9 cwt could not fully redress the balance: the top speed was about 70 mph instead of close to 90, and the smaller car lacked the sparkle of the larger one. Even when it went to OHV and 1776cc in late 1937, 65 bhp failed to compensate for a quarter-ton increase in weight: the performance was very little livelier than before. Besides, the big engine went up to 3½ litres and 125 bhp in the same year.

The various SS Jaguars were originally conceived as saloons, but they also appeared as drophead coupés and (in the case of the 2.5 litre) as an open four-seater. They were introduced in substantially similar form after the war; most manufacturers did this as a 'stop-gap' measure until new models were ready. The SS part of the name was however dropped, partly as no longer being appropriate and partly (as Sir William was later to say) because the Nazi SS had been 'a sector of the community not highly regarded . . .'

By late 1947, though, Jaguar had designed a new chassis with IFS to replace the old beam-axle cars; they also had the XJ and XK engines, as we have already seen.

What they did not have was any bodywork, because they had decided to buy in a pressed-steel body virtually complete, rather than use the old pre-war 'patchwork' methods. Because of the considerable lead time involved in getting Pressed Steel to make such a body, they decided on a compromise: they used the new chassis, the old 3½ litre push-rod engine, and an interim body made pretty much in their traditional way until they could get the new bodies. They decided against using the new engine in the car, because they wanted a striking modern body that was worthy of it; and the result was the Mk. V Jaguar – the original 'Wardour Street Rolls'. It was a big, handsome vehicle, also available as a very fine drophead. More than any other Jaguar to date, the Mk. V had 'space' as well as 'pace' and 'grace'. A top speed of 91 mph was pretty pacey, especially in the 1940s, and the appearance was impressive, even if it tended more to the imposing than to the graceful. There was also a 2½ litre version of the same car, with 102 bhp instead of 125 bhp and only about a 50 lb saving (across a total weight of a ton and a half) when compared with the 3½ litre; this was a clear case of 'the same, only less', and the 3½ litre cars always outnumbered the smaller ones by about 4:1.

There was no Mk. VI – Bentley were using that name – and the Mk. VII used both the new chassis and the XK engine (with 160 bhp) together with pressed steel bodywork in the modern idiom; the long, flowing curves of the Mk. VII would have been difficult, time-consuming, and weighty to achieve with the old patchwork-and-filler approach. It was introduced at the 1950 Motor Show at £988 basic, or £1275:19:6d with the infamous purchase tax.

It was a rather more rounded vehicle than the Mk. V, and perhaps less dignified, but it was still a very real alternative to a Rolls Royce for those whose pockets (or egos) did not stretch that far. With its very considerable size, it certainly possessed 'space' aplenty; and with the XK engine to enable its considerable 34½ cwt bulk to top 100 mph, no-one could deny that it possessed 'pace'; the only doubt, as with all of the very biggest Jaguars, was the grace. It was by no means ugly; but it was perhaps just a tiny bit vulgar. It was also the first Jaguar to offer an automatic gearbox, again with the American market in mind, in early 1953.

In 1954, the car was updated to the Mk. VIIM, with many minor styling changes (including wrap-around rear bumpers) and a 190 bhp version of the XK engine, raising the top speed slightly – even the automatic could manage 100 mph – and improving acceleration across the board. The Mk. VIII of 1956 was possibly less of a change than this, although slight changes to the cylinder head gave rather improved top-end performance (road tested at over 106 mph) and styling changes included a one-piece screen. The Mk. IX (1958) was a further logical development, but all the changes were under the skin: disc brakes were fitted, and the engine rose to 3.8 litres and 220 bhp, giving a remarkable top speed for so big and heavy a car of almost 115 mph – though fuel consumption had dropped from around 18 mpg in the Mk. VII to more like 15 mpg in the Mk. IX.

The 1962 Mk. X was a complete rethink of the big Jaguar theme, and it certainly was *big* – 16' 10" long, 6' 4" wide, and 1¾ tons in weight. The 265 bhp S-type engine could propel it at over 105 mph, albeit at a fuel cost of 13-15 mpg. Unlike the Mk. VII derivatives, it was of unitary construction, with IRS based on the E-type's. It was vast, it was fast, and (astonishingly, and despite fairly spectacular roll) it handled very well indeed. In 1966 it was renamed the 420G, with some detail changes, and until the arrival of the XJ-series saloons, it was something of a flagship in the Jaguar range. Although series production was discontinued in June 1970, it lives on in one way: with the wheelbase stretched 21", the Mk. X chassis still forms the basis for the enormous Daimler DS420 limousine, which fell to Jaguar when they took over that august firm in 1960.

Before going on to consider the XJ-series, though, we must return to 1955 to see the beginning of the 'baby' Jaguar saloons, the 2.4 and 3.4. They were of unitary construction from the start, with a very strong body whose looks were marred by the thickness of the window-frames and roof-pillars. The car was conceived as a real baby, perhaps using the 4-cylinder XJ engine, but in the interests of smoothness they chose instead a short-stroke version of the XK 3.4, with a capacity of only 2483cc, with mild cams and restrictive carburation to keep the power down to 112 bhp. With only 27 cwt to propel, this resulted in a car which would have been thought of as reasonably nippy – if it had not been a Jaguar. Cries for a 3.4 version were loud and immediate, especially from the United States, and early in 1957 these prayers were answered: despite an extra 1½ cwt, 210 bhp raised the top speed from just over 100 mph to just under 120 mph, and knocked the 0-60 mph time down from 14½ seconds to just over 9.

In 1959, the 2.4 and 3.4 were refined into Mk. II versions, and joined by a 3.8. The 2.4 received a modest increase in power, to 120 bhp, but this was somewhat offset by a 1½ cwt increase in weight. The real difference lay in the 3.8, with its 220 bhp (only 10 bhp more than the 3.4) and its 240 ft-lb of torque, a result of the B-type improved-port head; the 3.4 could only boast 216 ft-lb.

These are all delightful little cars, with quite astonishing performance: the 3.8 can reach 60 mph in 8½ seconds, 100 mph in 25 seconds, and go on to a top speed in excess of 125 mph. At exactly 1½ tons, fuel consumption ranges from about 16 mpg if driven hard to 18-20 mpg or slightly better if driven sensibly. The slimmer screen pillars give better visibility as well as better looks, and a good example of any of the breed remains an exhilarating car to this day, though naturally the 2.4 is rather lacking in urge when compared with the others. On the other hand, this smallest six is as smooth and sweet an engine as you could wish for – probably the smoothest of all Jaguar sixes, and that is saying something.

In 1967, the Mk. II became the 240 and 340, visibly cheaper than their previous selves: this was, of course, a 'softening up' for the XJ saloons which were to come. The 240 was finally discontinued in 1969, a few months after the 340; the 3.8 disappeared with the other Mk. II Jaguars in 1967.

Although in this book very little mention has been made of Daimler, they really deserve a place here because of the use of the Daimler 2½ litre V8 in the 2.4/3.4 bodyshell. A remarkably smooth little engine, it delivered 140 bhp, which made it a neat intermediate model between the 2.4 and the 3.8; it was also a good deal faster, at over 112 mph, than the 2.4. The story is that the Daimler 4½ litre V8 was tried in some of the larger Jaguars, and was so embarrassingly quick that it was killed off; certainly, with the V12 in the offing, it would have been foolish to tool up for the V8 – but it is still an interesting thought . . .

One last Jaguar saloon series which must be mentioned before we get on to the XJ series is the S-type/420. These were 'stretched' versions of the Mk. II, though the differences were more extensive than this might imply: they were not only bigger, but they also incorporated IRS. From the right angle, and in the right light, they look like slightly larger-than-usual Mk. IIs; on other occasions, they had something of the grossness of the Mk. X. They were intended as a bridge between the small Mk. II and the big Mk. X, and in that sense they were successful enough; but they are perhaps the least highly regarded of postwar Jaguar saloons, being neither one thing nor the other, neither as quick as a Mk. II nor as large and luxurious as a Mk. X. They were made from 1963 to 1968, though the Daimler Sovereign (which was pure 'badge engineering') survived until August 1969.

All of these Jaguars – large, medium, and small – were to be rendered obsolete at a stroke in 1968. In that year came the new XJ-series saloons, the definitive new Jaguars, which remain in production to this day.

In one sense, the car was completely new: apart from the time-honoured XK engine, it shared very few interchangeable components with previous Jaguars. In another sense, it was not new at all: there was little or nothing that was revolutionary about the XJ6 – except the way in which all the strictly conventional components were assembled into a single package which must rate as highly as any in the world for a combination of looks, comfort, speed, handling; you name it.

The styling was very recognisably Jaguar; it was the last Lyons-designed car, and it had every bit as much of his genius in it as the SS100 or the XK120. It was originally fitted with a choice of 2.8 or 4.2 litre XK engines, delivering 180 bhp and 245 bhp respectively, enough to propel over 33 cwt of car (just under 33 cwt for the 2.8) at 117 and 124 mph respectively, with 0-60 times of 11 sec and just under 9 sec. This is enough to 'see off' a very considerable number of sports cars, but even the XJ6 4.2

was not the fastest of the series: the very elegant pillarless coupé version, the XJ12C (later known as the XJ5.3C) was fitted with the V12 engine and could surpass 140 mph with ease – even though it was slowed down by a 3-speed automatic gearbox! The V12 is normally supplied with the automatic box, except in the XJ-S, but the immense power of the engine makes this fairly unimportant from the speed point of view. It does, however, mean that it is no longer as easy to 'steer with the accelerator' as it is with a manual transmission – and which is surely one of the pleasures of driving a very fast car.

For a short while (1973-75) the smaller-engined XJ6 was dropped, presumably because of demand for the more powerful cars, and when it reappeared it was as a 3.4 with a similar top speed but slightly better acceleration. Other significant changes to the car included the adoption of a new Model 12 Borg Warner box in 1970, and the addition of 4 inches to the wheelbase in 1972; at first, the long-wheelbase cars carried the suffix L to the model name, but within a couple of years the long chassis was to become standard, as it gave a useful increase in rear legroom with little or no penalty elsewhere.

One last note on the XJ-series saloons is that the fuel consumption varies dramatically according to the model and how it is driven. 'Pussyfooting' a 2.8 can lift you well over 20 mpg, but the same figure is about what you might expect for normal give-and-take driving. The 4.2 returns more like 15-16 mpg – you would be hard put to reach 20 – and the XJ12 commonly manages around 12 mpg, with perhaps 15 mpg to reward the careful driver. The interesting point here is not the economy from the driver's point of view – few Jaguar owners worry unduly about that – but the fact that it runs counter to all the trends of the 1970s, when a fear of burning petrol which verged upon paranoia seemed to envelop the world.

Although at the time of writing the XJ-series were the only Jaguar saloons, there are repeated rumours of new, small Jaguars in the tradition of the Mk. II; if and when these do come, they should certainly be interesting . . .

In view of Jaguar's sporting image, it would have been surprising if no-one had tried them in competition. In fact, there have been two separate strands of Jaguar racing and rallying; the use of more-or-less standard cars, with or without some degree of special preparation, and the built-for-racing cars, which have not been mentioned yet.

Jaguar's attitude towards competition has always been extremely hard-nosed: others might race for the fun of it, but Jaguar raced to sell cars. Often, they have given works support to private entrants whilst stopping short of paying for it all themselves. This first happened in the 1933 Alpine Rally, when they loaned four cars to private entrants, who then paid all their own expenses. Two of the four SS1 cars finished, but Jaguar learned a great deal at comparatively modest cost.

The SS100 enjoyed a fair amount of success before the war, with Tommy Wisdom gaining Best Overall Performance and a Glacier Cup (for a totally 'clean' run) at the 1936 Alpine Trial in a 2½ litre. With similar cars, F.J. McEvoy took a class win at the 1936 Marne Grand Prix at Rheims, and Casimiro d'Oliveira won the 1937 Vila Real race in Portugal outright. It was in the immediate post-war years, though, that the SS100 did best, in those curious days when the best of pre-war cars battled it out before the appearance of post-war new developments. Ian Appleyard (who was to marry Lyons' daughter) was a leading figure; he took eighth place in the 1947 Alpine trial and (with factory support) won the 1948 event, going on to come second in the 1949 Tulip Rally.

After the war, with rather more attention being paid to the sporting image, the story changed somewhat – it is interesting, incidentally, to note that from 1936 to 1940, only 265 SS100s appeared, as compared with over 14,000 Jaguar saloons, dropheads, and tourers. The XK120 was entered for the 1949 Daily Express Silverstone production car race; of three cars, one was delayed badly by a burst tyre, but the others finished first and second; a 1938 SS100 3½ litre was fifteenth!

In 1950/51, the basically production XK120 picked up a lot of victories and good places. Leslie Johnson took a fourth place at Palm Beach (the XK120s first real race), a fifth in the Mille Miglia, and was lying second at Le Mans at half distance when his clutch packed up. Lyons, who was there, was sufficiently impressed to give the go-ahead for a works car for the 1951 Le Mans on the spot! Stirling Moss won the Irish TT, with other Jaguar XK120s taking 1-2-3 class places and ensuring a team win; Phil Hill won at Palm Springs; the Daily Express race in 1950 saw Jaguars first, second, fourth, and fifth; and Ian Appleyard won the Alpine, collecting eight awards in the process; in 1951 he won in the Alpine, Tulip, and RAC rallies. In the same year, Cecil Vard took a Mk. V to third place in the Monte Carlo rally (he took fifth with the same car in 1953), and Claes and Ickx won the Rome-Liege rally.

Although all these wins might stir the soul of a European, or of an American enthusiast who followed racing closely, Lyons was aware that a Le Mans win would carry real prestige, even with those who knew very little about racing. Accordingly, the XK120 was extensively modified to produce the XK120C, universally known as the C-type. Despite the fracture of an oil pipe flange on two of the cars – a trivial fault which nevertheless put them out of the race, where Jaguars had been lying 1-2-3 – one survived and won outright at an average speed of 93.49 mph for 24 hours – just short of two-and-a-quarter *thousand* miles, in a solid day's driving. Moss broke the lap record repeatedly, leaving it at 105.2 mph. A privately entered XK120, in almost standard form, finished eleventh!

Other Jaguar successes included Moss' win in the Tourist Trophy (with a Jaguar class placing of 1, 2, 3) and two successes at Goodwood; that year, Jaguar won the Dewar Trophy for automotive achievement as well as (yet again) the Daily Express Silverstone meeting. The list of wins in lesser events is interminable, and 1951 also saw the formation of Ecurie Ecosse, a team of Scots enthusiasts, who were to drive Jaguars to many successes.

In 1952, the year began with a fourth place in the Monte Carlo Rally for Rene Cotton in his Mk. VII. The Silverstone race saw wins in the XK120, C-type, and Mk. VII for Moss. The Mille Miglia seemed almost within reach until Moss damaged his steering in an accident, and Le Mans was another disaster when last-minute alterations resulted in cooling problems; all three cars retired in the first hour.

By this time, the C-type had grown (much-needed) disc brakes, and Moss won the Rheims 12hr race in it a few weeks after the Le Mans fiasco; Ecurie Ecosse's XK120, driven by Scott-Douglas, was third. The C-type now became a catalogued production car.

In 1953 came another spectacular win at Le Mans. Mercedes did not bother to enter, feeling that they had proved themselves sufficiently in 1952, but the winning C-type won at an average race speed no less than 9 mph higher than the Mercedes the previous year! Behind the Rolt/Hamilton winning car came two more Jaguars, in second and fourth place.

For 1954, the D-type replaced the C-type; it was some 20 mph faster and much more stable, but teething troubles including loss of brakes and persistent misfiring meant that only one car finished, Rolt and Hamilton coming second in torrential rain; they also managed second place at Rheims. Silverstone was a small consolation prize – 1, 2, 3 for Mk. VII saloons with C-type engines – and in the following year the Mk. VIIs took the team prize at the Monte Carlo Rally, albeit fairly far down the field.

Like the C-type, the D-type became a production car; and like the C-type, some were put into street-legal trim and used on the road – a fascinating thought, as the C-type weighed exactly a ton and had at least 200 bhp at its command, whilst the D-type was 3 cwt lighter and had an extra 50 bhp. Top speeds were about 145 mph and 162 mph respectively.

The 1955 Le Mans 24 hrs was the scene of the horrific crash when a Mercedes left the track and ploughed into the crowd like a fireball – the body contained a good deal of magnesium – and killed 85 people. The Hawthorn/Bueb D-type won, but it was something of a hollow victory; in any case, if Mercedes had not withdrawn immediately, they might well have won. Phil Walters won the Sebring 12 hour race in a D-type, and the Silverstone event was the usual 1, 2, 3, this time with Mike Hawthorn as team leader.

In 1956, Ronald Adams started the year well by winning the Monte Carlo Rally in a Mk. VII, and D-types finished 1-2-3-4 at Rheims which was before Le Mans that year. In the big 24 hour race, though, the works Jaguars were all eliminated by minor faults and accidents which did not really reflect upon the car; but Ecurie Ecosse took a D-type across the line in first place, so it was still a Jaguar win.

This was really the last year of works Jaguar racing, even at Silverstone, where Ivor Bueb won in a Mk. VII (again!) despite a works team of 2.4 litre saloons; thereafter, Jaguar themselves were to concentrate on production and prototype road cars. Then, in 1957, a disastrous factory fire put an end to the D-type assembly line (and also to the very limited-production XKSS road car which was based on it).

Thereafter, it was up to the privateers to fly the Jaguar flag – which they did, with only a little help from the factory. The leading lights were David Murray's Ecurie Ecosse, and Briggs Cunningham.

Paradoxically, the best ever Le Mans for Jaguar was that first one after they had stopped works support. Ecurie Ecosse came in first, second, and third (Flockhart/Bueb winning), and other D-types came in fourth and sixth! This was the last truly great Jaguar racing year, though, because the dichotomy between fast road cars – which the Jaguars were, *par excellence* – and purpose-built sports/racing cars was becoming even more marked. On top of this, the 1958 international sports car racing championship specified an engine capacity limit of three litres – which did not suit the Jaguar engine at all well.

The Mk. II versions of the small saloons were very successful indeed as production car racers, and also in rallies, and they continued to be extremely competitive until the middle 1960s, when they were edged out of rallies by smaller, nimbler cars and out of saloon car racing by the American 'muscle cars', with sheer power which will probably never be surpassed in road cars.

It was not until the 1970s that Jaguar themselves returned to racing, though in the intervening years their cars had provided a great deal of fun for all concerned, and proved very competitive at club level. One of the most famous go-faster Jaguars was the lightweight E-type, with D-type cylinder head, petrol injection, alloy block, and body made of thinner steel and light alloy; 300 bhp was usual, with 344 bhp being achieved on some engines. These were never exactly production cars, and it is likely that no two were ever quite identical, but they were certainly very fast. They were not, however, in the same class as the Ferrari 250 GT or the Ford GT40, which marked the direction in which sports/racing cars were moving. Another interesting excursion was the 1965/66 XJ13 mid-engined car, with a 5-litre 4-cam V12. Strictly a one-off, it lapped the Motor Industry Research Association track at 161 mph, reaching 175 mph *en route;* but like the other mid-engined V8 of the time from Rover, it was to be stifled at birth. Rover fans say that the latter car was not pursued because it represented too much of a threat to the E-type!

In August 1974, British Leyland Inc. announced a plan to race V12 E-types in the Sports Car Club of America's production championship. A first time out win by Lee Mueller at Seattle astounded the cynics, whilst a day later Bob Tullius was leading at Watkins Glen when his gear lever broke off, which put him out of the race very effectively. During the rest of that season, Mueller and Tullius won most of the races they entered, but they did not amass enough points to win their class in the championship. In 1975, though, Tullius reached the Road Atlanta finals and won the championship, upon which British Leyland Inc. withdrew their support.

Again, in 1976, Ralph Broad of Broadspeed was invited by Jaguar to prepare an XJ12C for racing, as he had been suggesting for the previous couple of years: it was to contest the European Touring Car Race Championship, which was (and still is) a BMW playground. At Silverstone, the specially-built lightweight car with the go-faster V12 engine achieved the fastest practice time of the day, with a lead of better than two seconds over the fastest BMW, but was eventually put out of the race with a failed driveshaft – the same fault which was to beset the car in 1977 at Salzburgring, only its second appearance after the 1976 race because the intervening time had been devoted to development work. At Brno, the cars again proved very fast (170 mph on the straight, and new lap records), but again they had to retire. Their only real success of the season was a second place (to BMW) at the Nurburgring, and at the end of the season BL withdrew from racing.

The XJS was, however, campaigned with success by Bob Tullius; in 1977 he won five of the ten races he entered and won the Drivers' Championship; in 1978 he won both the Drivers' and Manufacturers' divisions of the Trans-Am championship. Perhaps this was what inspired Jaguar to think again, though it was not until 1983 that they announced that they had 'plans' to return to racing – though at the time of writing, the exact nature of the plans was unclear.

Or perhaps . . . one of the most spectacular achievements of the XJ-S was an outright win of the highly illegal Cannonball Run, a coast-to-coast race across open public roads in the USA. With a federal speed limit of 55 mph, the XJ-S averaged 87 mph: now that is *real* road-racing.

LYONS AND JAGUARS

Sir William Lyons has been mentioned at intervals throughout this book; and this is no surprise, for until his retirement he *was* Jaguar. In the early days, there was Bill Walmsley, but late in 1934 he left; he was far less interested than Lyons in running a large company, and had been leaving more and more of the day-to-day running of the firm to Lyons for a fair while previously. He was not without influence – it was probably his special order for two open two-seaters in 1934 for his personal use which inspired the SS90 and SS100 – but he spent more and more time with his beloved model railways, often having parts made up in the SS toolroom, much to Lyons' annoyance.

All of the motor moguls, whether heads of giant companies like Morris and Austin, or of smaller concerns such as Standard (Sir John Black) and Jaguar, seem to have been somewhat abrasive characters; some who dealt with them would be less charitable, and of some there has been bandying of words such as 'megalomania'. It would certainly not be unfair to say of Sir William that he was a man who liked his own way, and who was disinclined to suffer fools gladly; but this is one of the penalties for being right as often as Sir William was. One of the most interesting sidelights on the evolution of the motor industry, though, is the extent to which personal quarrels and enmities were involved, and how so many advances were due to a single key man.

Despite the heading 'Lyons and Jaguars', there is little need to continue at length about Sir William's contribution to the *marque*. It stemmed from a unique combination of business acumen and artistic talent; as a sculptor of motor cars, from the original Swallow bodies to the XJ-series saloons, he has had no equal. Some of the Italian stylists may be better known, but (unlike Sir William) most of them have made some fairly hideous mistakes which, moreover, they have displayed with pride at various motor shows; Sir William, less given to 'design exercises', has got it right far more often. The way in which he worked, strictly by eye with a metalsmith interpreting his ideas, has already been mentioned; and the dire results when a non-Lyons Jaguar appeared in the form of the XJ-S are well known.

Apart from Sir William, one of the most important names to have been associated with Jaguar was probably Harry Weslake. An Exeter man with a genius for engine development via gasflow studies, it is said that the first contact between him and Jaguar arose because he had fallen out with Cecil Kimber of MG, and was looking for a way to spite him by producing a faster car for someone else! Certainly, the MG SA was the nearest thing to a direct competitor to the SS Jaguars – but it lacked both the Lyons and the Weslake touches. It was Weslake who was responsible for a great deal of the XK engine, too.

Another major character was William Heynes, who came to Jaguar from Humber. As well as the engine work, he was responsible for many suspension innovations including the use of torsion bars (he had long been an admirer of the *Traction avant* Citroën). Unlike many of the other characters in the Jaguar drama, he was not given to making enemies, and is very highly regarded as the author of many serious and well-thought-out papers on engineering topics.

To bring in other names such as Wally Hassan, 'Lofty' England, and others would be fruitless; any of them could be a fit subject for a biography, and justice cannot be done to them here. It is still worth pointing out, though, that the success of Jaguar was due in very large measure to a fairly small number of enthusiasts, who were sufficiently fiery that they could carry others at Jaguar with them; more than most motor manufacturers, Jaguar is very much a place where there is a feeling of working together to make a car. This applied to a certain extent even in the dark days when the dead hand of British Leyland tried to suppress all make names, and get the cars known as 'Leyland', and with the re-emergence of Jaguar as a clear marque, it is on the up-and-up.

The politics of Jaguar's existence have always been complicated. In the 1930s, Sir John Black of Standard (who supplied chassis and engines) wanted a part of the action; but Sir William (or plain William, as he then was) preferred to be on his own. After the war, when Lyons accepted Black's offer of some Standard engine-manufacturing plant with great alacrity before Black could change his mind, Black was so piqued that he determined to use the newly-acquired Triumph name on cars to out-Jaguar Lyons himself; but although the Roadster made more than a nod in that direction, the subsequent TR sports cars were very much smaller, slower, cheaper, and more spartan than the XK-series (though still fine cars in their own right), and the saloons similarly carried the idea of a well-made, well-finished car a few notches down market from Jaguar.

Had Sir William's only son not been so tragically killed in a motor accident on his way to Le Mans in 1955, the Jaguar name might just have continued independently; but in the economic thinking of the 1960s, 'bigger was better', and he saw the best chance for Jaguar's survival in integration with a larger group; and in 1966 the firm merged with the giant British Motor Corporation, itself compounded chiefly of Morris and Austin. Cynics may say that the government of the day encouraged such mergers because it would make nationalisation easier in due course (which it did), and there is a certain amount of truth in this; but for a while, it really did look as if economies of scale were going to be that important, and this was presumably what settled Sir William's mind. He was very careful to retain control of the company-within-a-company, though, to ensure that Jaguar remained more than just another badge to be stuck on whatever car the combine wanted to endow with the Jaguar image – the fate, for example, of the MG name.

What had not been foreseen was the grand merger between British Motor Holdings and Leyland Motors to form BLMC in 1968, which was to result in 1972 in the disappearance of Jaguar Cars Limited. Those dark years of the 1970s are now best left unremembered, but the tide turned in 1977 when Michael Edwardes headed the company and the Ryder Plan was discarded. It was to be 1980, though, before Jaguar was to re-emerge properly as a company with an identifiable head.

Aided by a government with a pronounced lack of faith in state control of industry, John Egan – now Sir John – took the helm of a company whose image had become somewhat tarnished. Quality and efficiency once again became the keywords as Jaguar began its long haul back to the top of an ever more competitive world automotive industry.

In the ensuing years productivity has more than trebled and quality improved beyond recognition. Indeed, such was the transformation that when the company's shares were floated on the London Stock Exchange in 1984, investor confidence in the firm's future ensured that the floatation was a resounding success, with the offer being over-subscribed eightfold.

Marred only by the sad death of Sir William Lyons in February 1985, Jaguar's history since privatisation has been nothing short of remarkable. Major investment has been made in plant and research, while product quality and design have all undergone considerable improvement. Most recently, the model range has grown to include the luxurious and exciting XJ-S Convertible as well as the new, award-winning XJ6 Saloon range.

The completely redesigned XJ6 range of luxury saloons, the company's 'bread and butter' cars, appeared in 1987. Gone were the stalwart XK engines that had served the Series III cars so well, and in came the lightweight, more powerful, but also more economical 2.9 litre 2 valve single cam and and 3.6 litre 4 valve per cylinder all-aluminium engines. The culmination of a seven-year, £200 million development programme, these are the cars on which the success of the company so heavily depends. Complementing the XJ6s are the Sovereign and Daimler models, with the Sovereign available with both engine variants while the Daimler is available only with the larger engine.

For those with a taste for sheer power coupled with unrivalled luxury, the Sovereign V12 and Daimler Double Six range continued unchanged into the 1988 season. In true Jaguar tradition, the grace of the classic Series III body remained married to the pace provided by the muscle-packed 5.3 litre V12 unit.

Previewed at the 1988 Geneva International Motor Show, the XJ-S Convertible became the company's first full convertible model since the historic E-Type roadster. Built to the exacting standards of the company's other luxury cars, the Convertible delivers electrifying performance thanks to its V12 engine, and boasts as standard equipment anti-lock braking, electrically operated hood, air conditioning, as well as the luxury of a traditional leather and walnut interior. Together with the Coupé and Cabriolet versions, this car possesses the sort of head-turning looks one has come to expect of a Jaguar thoroughbred.

But what of motorsport? It was to the delight of all true enthusiasts that John Egan announced the marque's return to racing in early 1983. Powered by a development of the V12 engine, it was to be just a matter of time before the cars were answering those sceptics who considered Porsche to be invincible. Under the management of Tom Walkinshaw Racing, the Silk Cut Jaguars have notched up an amazing string of successes, beginning with victory for the 6.0 litre XJR-6 in the Silverstone 1000 in 1986 and continuing into the memorable 1987 season when the World Sportscar Championship was claimed by the superbly-prepared XJR-8s, winning eight of the ten rounds that year. The XJR-9s of the 1988 season made headlines with their fine victories at Daytona for the Castrol Racing team, where they broke an 11-year Porsche winning streak, followed by victory for the Silk Cut outfit at the world's premier sportscar event – Le Mans. Driven by two Britons and a Dutchman, the No 2 Silk Cut Jaguar made it the sixth-ever win at Le Mans for the marque, and the first since the memorable 1957 race when Jaguar had claimed the first four places.

In May 1988 Jaguar announced yet another exciting joint venture with Tom Walkinshaw Racing. Initially producing some 500 JaguarSport cars per annum, the company intends to expand production to about 2,500 high performance and sporting derivatives of the Jaguar range of saloon and XJS sports cars for sale to enthusiasts worldwide. With the commitment to racing in terms of investment and R&D that Jaguar continues to show, the big cats will surely remain in the sporting limelight for years to come.

The Jaguar name first appeared in 1935 on a re-designed model range produced by S.S. Cars Ltd. The name had been chosen to distinguish the new, higher performance product from its somewhat pedestrian – if excitingly-styled – predecessors. Thanks to the development work carried out on the Standard power unit and chassis by Harry Weslake and William Heynes, the performance of the new models was considerably improved. Shown *these pages* is a 1937 SS 100 two-seater open sports car, which was fitted with a 2.5 litre straight-six using the Weslake-designed head. The car's body construction remained traditional, consisting of an aluminium skin over an ash frame.

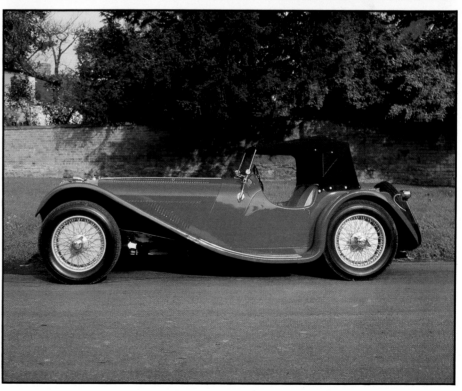

Conventionally styled and outwardly similar to the SS 90, the SS 100 *these pages* was in effect William Lyons' first true production sports car. With its elegant, sweeping lines, excellent handling and lively performance, the car attracted considerable Press interest. In standard road-trim the new car was capable of around 95 mph and a 0-60 time of 12.8 seconds.

Not only was the Jaguar a superb performer on the roads – it was soon to prove its worth in international competitions, notably in the Alpine Trial and the Marne Grand Prix at Rheims in 1936 and at Vila Real in 1937 – successes that were to enhance the firm's standing as a builder of fine cars.

Although production at SS Cars during the war years was given over to armament contracts, Lyons and his team continued to plan ahead. By the time hostilities were over a new engine and chassis were already taking shape, and they were to form the basis of the planned post-war luxury saloon. The Mark V *these pages,* launched in 1948, was intended as a stop-gap model. It used the old 2.6 and 3.5 litre pushrod engine and a body that was reminiscent of the pre-war cars, but mounted on the new chassis and suspension. The new ohc power unit was being reserved for a totally new Jaguar, which was to boast a truly new body shape.

The new XK engine, on which the company was pinning its postwar hopes, was first fitted in the XK 120 sportscar of 1948. Encouraged by its performance and racing successes, Jaguar Cars developed a lightweight competition model – the C type – with victory at Le Mans as the ultimate objective. Three cars were entered in the 1951 race, which resulted in a convincing win for the C type of Whitehead and Walker. Shown *these pages* is a 1952 car from Ecurie Ecosse.

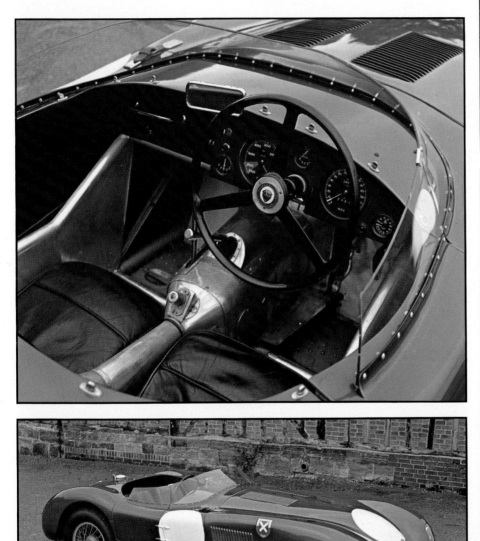

JWS 353

The XK 140, shown *these pages* in roadster form, was launched in 1954 as a replacement for the now ageing 120. The old body shape was retained but exterior trim was altered, notably the bumpers and radiator grille. The 190 bhp engine that had been a special on the 120 now became standard, and was repositioned to improve handling and increase interior space. Rack and pinion steering, as used on the C type, replaced the old recirculating ball set-up.

The legendary XK 120, which appeared in 1948, was originally intended as a test-bed for the new 3442 cc dohc XK engine. William Lyons is reputed to have designed its classic body shape in less than two weeks. The car used the chassis and suspension that had been developed for the proposed Mark VII saloon. Originally introduced as an open two-seater, the car was later to become available in both drophead and fixed head coupé forms. The earlier versions of the car were fitted with aluminium bodies but in 1950 these were superseded by a pressed steel shell which, although outwardly identical, was radically different under the skin. Wire wheels became a popular option in 1951, the year that the fixed head model *these pages* appeared. The fixed head variant boasted the more luxurious interior appointments of the saloons; wider doors and a roofline that was fractionally higher than that of the roadster with its hood raised. Although all this led to an increase in weight, the FHC suffered little in terms of performance: it was still capable of 120 mph and had a 0-60 time of 9.9 seconds.

The long awaited Mark VII saloon illustrated *these pages,* with its race-proved engine, thoroughly tested chassis and torsion bar suspension and new servo assisted brakes, was launched at the London Motor Show in October 1950. Dressed in its spectacular, flowing bodywork that had been designed by Lyons and built by the Pressed Steel Company, the car was the sensation of the show, and at a basic price of under £1000 it was in a class of its own. The combination of grace, pace and space that the new car offered made it irresistible, and at the American launch that followed, orders exceeded all expectations. To further enhance its appeal with American buyers automatic transmission was offered as an option in 1954 and an overdrive gearbox followed later that year.

Largely of monocoque-type construction, the D-type Jaguar *these pages* was a further development of the already successful C-types. Dry sump lubrication, all round disc brakes and a superbly streamlined body that was considerably lighter than its predecessor's helped the cars achieve some notable victories, including the first four places and a sixth at the 1957 Le Mans event, in which five of the cars had been entered.

After 4 years of faithful service, the Mark VII was given a face-lift and appeared, in September 1954, as the Mark VII M *these pages*. The car's front now sported new headlights and flashing indicators were fitted into the wings. Fog lamps were moved outside the body shell, their original place taken by a pair of horn grilles. Changes were also made in the power department with engine output raised from 160 to 190 bhp, and gearbox ratios made closer. The alterations resulted in an increased top speed and improved fuel consumption. The suspension was modified to reduce the amount of roll on cornering.

Compared to its XK 120 counterpart, the XK 140 fixed-head coupé *pictured here* was a relatively roomy car. The roofline had been extended back by some 7 inches and this, combined with the increased space due to a repositioned engine, meant that the car's rear seats could serve a useful purpose.

Despite the fact that Jaguar Cars Ltd showed their commitment to racing with the continued development of such cars as the D-type, it was the privately entered cars rather than the works team that took the lion's share of the racing honours. Jaguar themselves pulled out of competition in 1956 but the D-types continued to notch-up spectacular wins for some four more years.

Power output from the D-type's engine was gradually increased over the years and fuel injection as well as various body and chassis modifications helped make the cars even faster. Shown *above* is the normally aspirated engine of a 1955 car. The bulge behind the driver's head *right* houses the fuel filler cap and on later cars this headfairing was extended into an integral fin that increased stability.

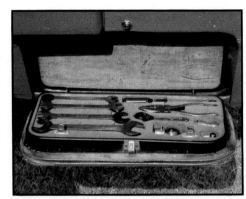

In 1956 the Mark VII M *far left, bottom left and bottom right* was replaced by the short-lived Model VIII. A one-piece screen and minor trim changes distinguished the new car and a new cylinder head boosted performance. The Mark IX of 1959 looked identical to the VIII but disc brakes, power steering and the 3.8 litre engine that had been used on the D-types after 1955 now became standard.

With the exception of the XJ6, the compact Mark II Jaguar, which was available with three engine options, was the company's most successful saloon; both in terms of numbers produced and the run of competition victories. Shown *this page* is a 3.4 litre model from 1963, which bears a remarkable resemblance to the XK 150S *facing page*. With its enlarged 3.8 litre engine, the 150S is generally considered the finest car of the XK sports line.

Last in the series of XK sports cars, the XK 150 was launched in 1957. The shape was noticeably different from its predecessor's: the waist-line was made higher, a curved one-piece screen was fitted and the radiator grille reverted to the style used on the 120. Disc brakes became standard and the new B type head improved performance in the mid-range.

Enthusiasts were quick to notice the potential of the compact Mark I and II saloons and the practice of improving their performance soon became commonplace. Specialist firms such as John Coombs, who had gained considerable racing experience with these cars, offered an 'improvement' service which transformed an already fast car into a really powerful machine. Illustrated is a 1962 3.8 litre Mark II which has undergone the Coombs treatment.

Bonnet straps, multi-slatted louvres, modified rear wheel arches and a protective grille over the headlights distinguish this Coombs conversion. Under the skin the changes were invariably more radical and could include such things as: increased compression ratios, a full gas flow head, new carburettors, steering box, exhaust and modified suspension. The racing successes of such Coombs cars, notably at the hands of Roy Salvadori, were considerable.

Looking remarkably similar to the D-type whose monocoque construction it had inherited, the magnificent E-type was unveiled at the Geneva Motor Show in 1961. The 3.8 litre engine and gearbox were basically those used in the XK 150S, but here was a car with an up-to-the-minute shape that was capable of a staggering 150 mph. Illustrated is a 1962 Series I fixed-head coupe.

Designed for economy rather than performance the 2.4 litre straight six XK engine as fitted to the Mark II *these pages* was capable of a top speed of around 93 mph. True enthusiasts, however, expected something more from a Jaguar and tended to favour the larger units, particularly the 3.8, which could cut the 2.4's 0-60 time of 17.5 seconds in half.

Now over twenty years old, the E-type is still a stunning 'good-looker' with performance to match. When it appeared, however, its impact can well be imagined. What amazed the *cognoscenti* even more than its pace was its superb handling and road-holding, due in no small part to the completely new independent rear suspension designed by Heynes. Here was a car that could be driven, even by the inexperienced, in considerable safety and comfort. Pictures show a 1965 Series I 4.2 litre E-type roadster, the larger engine having been introduced the previous year.

A new all-synchromesh gearbox, new seats, clutch and exhaust accompanied the arrival of the E-type's enlarged 4.2 litre engine. Acceleration times improved fractionally and increased torque coped with the unit's additional weight but top speed remained at 150 mph.

Like its sporting predecessors, the E-type was soon to bare its teeth on the racing track. Despite the encouragement of a victory in its first event at the hands of Graham Hill, however, it soon became obvious that more development work was needed if the cars were to challenge the near supremacy of the Ferrari 250 GT on the international scene. The E-type's major successes came in modsports competitions and in SCCA production sports car races in the United States.

Powered by either the 3.4 or 3.8 litre versions of the trusty 6 cylinder engine, the S type of 1963 was designed to complement the existing Mark II and Mark X ranges. Somewhere between the two in terms of size and luxury, the new model retained the features of the smaller car at the front while sporting the extended rear section of the Mark X.

Slim-line bumpers, differently positioned side lights and indicators, and re-designed rear wheel arches without valances were the less obvious differences between the S type and the Mark II. Rear suspension followed the pattern set by the Mark X, this being an independent coil spring and damper arrangement rather than leaf springs as featured on the Mark II. The two engine options were the same 3.4 and 3.8 units as on the smaller car but because of the increased weight, performance was down fractionally. Internally the car received some of the luxury Mark X treatment. The photographs *on these pages* show a 3.4 litre 1966 registered S type.

Still a Series I E-type, but considerably longer than the roadster and hard-top coupé, the 2+2 of 1966 added a degree of practicality to the car's unquestioned panache.

Here was an E-type that even the family man (or woman) could indulge in.

Apart from the 2+2's extended wheelbase, the height had been increased by some 2 inches over that of the hard top coupé, and doors were widened considerably to enable rear passenger access. When not in use, the rear seats could be folded down to give useful stowage space. Mechanical changes on the new car were minimal but automatic transmission became an option not available on any of the shorter models. A weight increase of 2.5 cwt took its toll on both acceleration times and maximum speed, with the 0-60 mph time now 8.9 sec, as opposed to 7 sec on the coupé.

It is a fitting tribute to the much admired Mark II saloon that well preserved examples can command a higher price today than they did when they first left the factory gates. Their incredible smoothness, comfort and fleetness of foot have guaranteed these cars a place in the history of the motor car. Pictures show a pristine example of the 2.4 litre version.

Above and left: Covered headlights, small air intake and triple windscreen wipers
identify this 1967 roadster as a Series I variant.

Beauty has rarely been skin deep on cars bearing the Jaguar name and with the E-type it is only with the hood raised that one can appreciate fully the skill and artistry that has gone into its creation. The picture *top left* shows the gleaming camshaft covers, aluminium induction manifold and triple SU carburettors of the superb 4.2 litre, six cylinder engine.

Shown *these pages* is the rather scarce E-type that came to be knowns as the 'Series 1½'. It preceded the Series 2 by some months and incorporated some of the features that were to appear on the future model. Outwardly, the open headlights were new, but triple wipers and the small intake opening from the Series 1 remained.

Cosmetic changes, such as new bumpers and a radiator grille, distinguished the Series 3 E-type. More drastically, however, the track had been widened and wider tyres fitted, necessitating flared wheel arches front and rear. The roadster *these pages* now adopted the longer 2+2 wheelbase and the 5.3 litre V12 engine ousted the straight-six as the standard power unit.

Generally considered to be the most significant model ever produced by Jaguar, the XJ6, which appeared in 1968, was to become part of a rationalization plan that witnessed the gradual demise of all other saloon models. Two engine options were initially offered – the 4.2 and a 2.8 litre version of the straight-six XK unit.

Enthusiastic press reports and considerable consumer interest soon meant that demand far outstripped supply for a car that had been almost four years in the making. Shown *these pages* is a 4.2 litre 1972 model that, with the introduction of updated versions, later became known as the Series 1.

Shown *these pages* is the famous lightweight E-type that was raced by the German duo of Peter Lindner and Peter Nocker. Only 12 of these special, aluminium bodied competition machines were ever built, and this one, with its modified Sayer tail section, boasted one of the most potent XK engines ever to have powered an Etype.

Powered by a fuel injected 3.8 litre engine which made use of an aluminium block and could deliver 344 bhp, the Lindner/Nocker competition E-type was fitted with a five speed ZF gearbox. Top speed of this much modified car, with its aerodynamically designed rear *facing page,* was in the region of 170 mph.

The 2+2 E-type *these pages* shared the improvements made to the remainder of the line with the introduction of the Series 2. Additionally, however, the angle of the windscreen was altered by bringing its base further forward and thus improving the car's appearance. Wire wheels were retained as a standard on all E-types until the introduction of wider tyres on the Series 3 in 1971.

In 1966 the venerable Mark II was put through an economizing process with plastic taking over from leather as the seating material and fog lamps supplanted by grilles. The following year further changes were made and the Mark II proper was discontinued in favour of the new 240 and 340 models. These incorporated the economies made on the II and also adopted the S-type's slim line bumpers. The 240 engine received a redesigned cylinder head and new carburettors while the 340 unit remained essentially the same. The 340 *left and above* was dropped from the range on the appearance of the XJ6 but the 240 *far left, top left and facing page* remained.

The original E-type range was to undergo a number of changes and improvements before it became the Series 2 in 1968. This updated version *these pages* sported a considerably enlarged air intake, new side/indicator light cluster as well as the open headlights which had appeared a little earlier. In the engine compartment new carburettors were fitted to models destined for the U.S. market. These reduced power but helped the car comply with newly introduced emission controls.

Above and left: a 1970 4.2 litre Series 2 E-type roadster.

Originally intended as an option on the E-type, the 4.2 litre engine, first fitted in 1964, soon supplanted the old 3.8 litre version. The larger unit was basically as before, but now received a new crankshaft and block. Maximum power remained unchanged at 265 bhp but torque was increased considerably.

Shown *these pages* with both its hood down and with the hard-top fitted, the open two-seater is probably the most exciting of the body options that were available on the E-type. In its Series 2 incarnation its production figures outstripped those of the 2+2 and were almost double those of the fixed-head coupe.

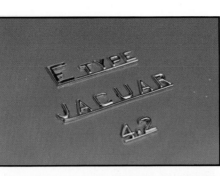

Increased demands on the E-type's 4.2
litre engine made by the American
pollution laws, and the consequent
downturn in performance, hastened the
introduction of an all new V12 engine.
Capacity of the aluminium unit, which
used a single overhead camshaft per bank
of cylinders, was 5.3 litres. This exciting
addition to the Jaguar range was unveiled
in 1971 in the considerably altered Series 3
E-type. Illustrated is a 1975 V12-powered
roadster, the air intake grille providing
instant Series 3 identification.

The 3.8 litre Mark X replaced the ageing Mark IX in 1961. Three years later this huge and luxurious saloon's engine was changed in favour of the 4.2 litre powerplant that was being used in the E-type. The 420 G *these pages,* essentially a Mark X with minor trim changes, made its debut in 1966. The G suffix distinguishes it from the smaller-bodied 420.

Other marques have laid claim to such lofty titles as 'The Standard of the World' and 'The World's Best Car' but Jaguar, in their own unassuming but self-assured way, have let the motorists discover the merits of their cars for themselves. There is little doubt that the majestic XJ6, shown *these pages* in 4.2 litre Series 1 guise, can be compared very favourably, in terms of handling, luxury and speed, with cars costing considerably more.

Consistent upgrading, production changes and modifications are something that Jaguar have practiced on all their ranges and the XJ saloons have been no exception. Feedback from customers and criticism by motoring correspondents is always taken seriously and, where possible, efforts are made to improve the car. The XJ range has to date gone through fairly drastic alteration, not because of any inherent faults but simply to keep the cars abreast of new developments and prevent them from dating.

In its present Series 3 form the XJ saloon is now available with 3.4 and 4.2 sixes and the 5.3 litre V12 engine. The 2.8 option was dropped in 1973. The long wheelbase variant was introduced in 1972 as the XJ6 L, and the longer shape was later adopted as standard on all the cars. The illustrations show a Series 3 4.2 litre XJ6 with its new-style radiator grille, rear light cluster, door handles, bumpers and wheels. Subtle body changes have given the cars an increased sleekness and grace.

Shown *these pages* is an independent but nonetheless stylish estate car modification based on the superb V12 powered XJS HE. Converted by Lynx Engineering and dubbed the Eventer, the car's advertising literature claims a combination of "extra space with amazing grace and thrilling pace." There can be little doubt that for the motorist who requires estate car capacity and sports car performance, the Eventer offers the ultimate solution.

The XJS was introduced in 1975 as a direct replacement for the E-type which, it was felt, had reached the ultimate stage of refinement in Series 3 form. A hard top design was decided on because of legislation that, at the time, was expected to affect the American market. To minimize development costs, the mechanics of the new car were to be based on the already proven XJ saloon and the 5.3 litre V12 engine. The new car's shape met with a mixed reception and many enthusiasts, who had

expected something as outwardly sporting as the E-type, refused to accept the addition to the family as a true Jaguar. With a shell design by Lyons and Sayer, performance equal to that of the E-type and comfort and handling in the XJ saloon class, the XJS is, without doubt, in the best tradition of the marque. Shown *top left and right and facing page* is the standard XJS HE and *above left and right* a Lynx Engineering Spyder conversion.

In 1977 CAR magazine awarded the the Daimler Double Six Vanden Plas the ultimate accolade: 'The Best Car in the World'. Arguably, in its 1983 guise the XJ12 (these pages) was even better. Equipped with the HE high efficiency version of the V12 5.3 litre engine that employed redesigned cylinder heads, the car returned improved fuel consumption figures as well as an increase in performance over its predecessors.

Facing page: a suitably regal setting for the magnificent XJ-S Coupé. Originally available only with the formidable 5.3 litre V12 engine (above) that has served Jaguar so ably since its introduction on the E-type in 1971, the Coupé is now also offered with the all-aluminium AJ6 3.6 litre engine developed for the new XJ6 range. In its highly tuned state, and bored out to a massive 7 litres, the V12 engine propels the XJR-9 racers up to 230 miles per hour.

Whether in Cabriolet (facing page) or Coupé (above) form, the XJ-S is undoubtedly one of the world's most attractive cars. Long and low, the V12 powered models match the electrifying top speeds that were attainable in the fastest of the E-types, while offering the comfort and luxury one has come to expect of Jaguar saloons. With its accent on refinement, the XJ-S boasts a standard of handling that eclipses its rather more Spartan sporting forebear.

Headlight treatment distinguishes the Sovereign (above) from the standard XJ6 (facing page). Both cars are offered with the option of either the 2.9 or 3.6 litre engine and five speed manual or four speed automatic transmission. Suspension modifications have meant that the latest XJ6 range offers an even better ride than the Series 3 cars, while the interior finish is vintage Jaguar, with wood veneer and a choice of leather or cloth upholstery. ABS braking and air conditioning are standard features on the Sovereign and Daimler variants.

Facing page: a classic setting for a classic car – the Sovereign in Rome's Piazza Navona.
Above: the Sovereign's flight deck, with its luxurious walnut and leather finish. Sovereign
and Daimler models boast a sophisticated audio system that delivers 80 watts of pure
sound through 6 speakers.

Time-honoured radiator grille embellishment identifies the Daimler (above) – top model in the XJ6 range. Available only with the larger 3.6 engine, the car offers as standard equipment the optional extras available on the XJ6 and Sovereign. Facing page: (top left) a cut-away drawing of the new all-aluminium 2.9 litre straight six engine, with its 'May' high efficiency combustion chambers, as available on the Jaguar XJ6 and Sovereign. Bottom right: the interior of the Sovereign (top right). Bottom left: the boot of a Jaguar XJ6 2.9.

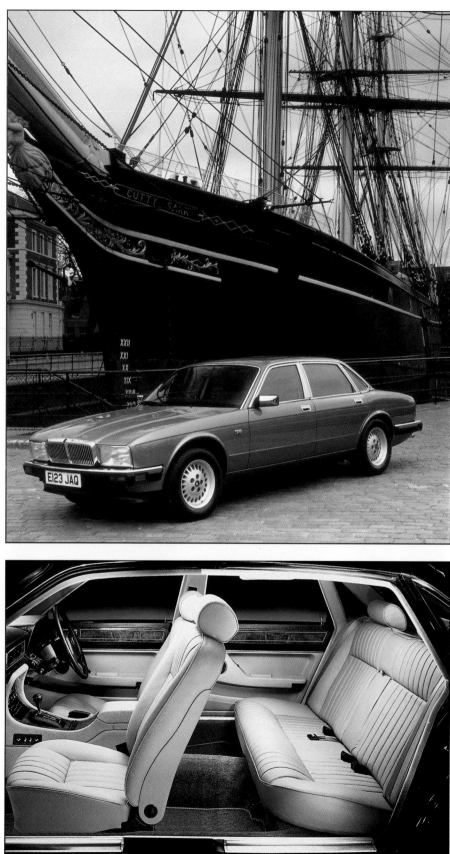

Equally at home on the autobahn or in Amsterdam, the steel-wheeled Jaguar XJ6 3.6 litre (above) draws admiring glances wherever it goes. Showing its race-bred lines in the pits at Le Mans (facing page) is a 3.6 litre XJ-S Coupé, with an XJR Silk Cut Jaguar in the background.

Under the management of Tom Walkinshaw Racing, Jaguars have once more gained their share of laurels on race tracks all over the world. Whether sporting Castrol Racing or Silk Cut livery, the cars have enjoyed considerable success. 1987 will long be remembered as the year when the XJR-8s captured the world championship, winning eight of the ten events that year, and recording a memorable 1-2 at Fuji (facing page bottom right). At Daytona (facing page bottom left), the opening event of the IMSA championships, in January 1988, it was the No. 60 XJR-9 driven by Nielsen, Boesel and Brundle that took the flag after a gruelling 24 hours, forcing a Porsche into second place for the first time in eleven years. Meanwhile, at Jarama (facing page upper right) in Spain in March of the same year, Cheever and Brundle kept the powerful Sauber Mercedes at bay. Victories at Monza, Silverstone, Le Mans, Brands Hatch and Fuji followed, and an outstanding season culminated in a second successive victory in the world team championship as well as top honours for Martin Brundle in the drivers' championship. Above: the No. 3 Silk Cut Jaguar at Le Mans.

Latest in the long line of exotics from the Jaguar stable is the beautiful XJ-S Convertible (these pages). Unveiled at the Geneva International Motor Show in March of 1988, the car boasts a power-operated hood, anti-lock braking, air conditioning and the super-smooth V12 engine. Overleaf: the XJ-S in Coupé form.